AF382489

Maher Asaad Baker

Chords of Change

ISBN Softcover: 978-3-384-40454-1

ISBN Hardback: 978-3-384-40455-8

ISBN E-Book: 978-3-384-40456-5

Cover image designed by Freepik

Contents

Introduction

Throughout history, music has been a significant factor to the formation of a Lithuanian cultural memory. National songs and dances, reflecting people's ambassadors, are intrinsically in the history of the nation, as the extended relatives from one generation to the other. Precisely, there is evidence that during the time of occupation and repression, musical culture and especially singing contributed crucially to sustaining the Lithuanian identity.

Including songs of prehistoric ceremonial and contemporary Lithuanian rock and pop, the music of the country and its nation sings out. They symbolize concepts and convey stories particular to Lithuanian practices, history and identity, about the connections between tradition, art and identity.

Based on the history of the Lithuanian people, folk music serves as the essential foundation of the state identities – icons of songs and instruments evoke timeless touches with the ground, legends and existence. Prehistoric and medieval beginnings of the Baltic peoples through the evolution of regional and national identities embracing centuries of history up to the arrival of the twenty-first-century breakaway states. These musical varieties are the clones of the country's historical and geographical evolution and a fundamental Lithuanian identity.

Different ethnographic territories – Dzūkija, Suvalkija, Aukštaitija and Žemaitija – have different sets of material linked to languages, geography and occupation. There are links tying them together into a single strident Lithuanian sound – emotional and skilfully sentimental, full thereby full of harmonies and inventive polyphonic singing. These unifying musical qualities appear to reflect some of the essence of the Lithuanian spirit.

Many archaic songs are the genuine echoes of pre-Christian Lithuania. Ceremonial and sung pieces connected to solstices, harvests and worship of natural elements are still prehistoric Baltic in character though this has been overlaid with later material. These services of tribal past define the symbolic Lithuanian culture. Again, traditional instruments also relate past and present – various kinds of percussive instruments like kanklės (Baltic psalteries), lamzdeliai (reed pipes) and skudučiai (panpipes) have accompanied the most archaic segments of Lithuanian nationality.

Brought into the folk circuit later, including violins, cymbals and accordions helped augment a part more folk music during the wearing and Baroque periods. However, Lithuania did not simply digest external forms – it engaged with foreign influences in a proactive manner and on its own account. The improvisational, fresh quality to Lithuanian folk music shows that the nation's culture, which is established in its roots, is constantly unstatic and adjusting over the different time periods. Music interchange happens through the process of continuous cultural development rather than the throwing-off process.

Adverse historical influences such as the Soviet occupation during 1944-1990 also did not expel conventional arts. In fact, folk music assumed rebel meanings as citizens' uprising after the restriction of public performances by the communists. Folk instruments or songs before the Soviet regime were equal to the political act of preserving national identity.

The continued viability of folk arts means that they are at the core of a definition of what it means to be Lithuanian. Traditional forms include relationships between land, ancestors, values, poetry and identity, which differs from other nations and is Lithuanian. People convey coalescence of the past and brotherhood in the present with one another and with the deceased. Nonetheless, musical heritage in Lithuania continued to thrive actively, not as a museum relic, but as an active organism which carries the genes of a nation.

Music production reflects and entertains needs beyond people's creativity – it addresses a fundamental social and religious concept of inclusion in Lithuanian culture. Practices distort music into a form of congregational celebration of a group's beliefs and norms.

The multipart singing tradition that has UNESCO status is best proved by Lithuania, where singing is of communal importance. Syncopated Villagers songs performed include imitative part-song in two, three or four parts, a cappella. Being like discussions, the chorus is a combined voice that brings out the individual sounds into a compound poly rhythmic discussion. The effect says that consonance arises out of dissonance; the resulting clarity defines the stated compositional flexibility of the piece meaning that every participant offers his or her melodic interpretation of the material. Symbolically, this co-ordination translates into multipart singing as the best representation of togetherness as well as identification with the nation's goals.

Yet another important instrument connecting performers to the listeners is the call and response form. Singers edit the refrain lines to mean that listeners should give choral responses. This literate dialogue effectively deconstructs the wall between artists and the audience – everybody in nearly every picture partakes in a collective rite in music-making. Therefore, Lithuanian folk concerts have gostunamativeness that make them unique not only when performing on a big festival stage. Contemplations are crowded with stars dancing bodily close with the attendants performing beat or backup vocals. Musical communication creates a fleeting bond with everyone attending, using shared emotions from the sounds of the Lithuanian spirit.

Therefore, both public concerts, and private musical events cultivate togetherness. Sėdėjimai is an unusual kind of social meal which reflects the spirit of joy, folk music such as accordions and a considerable amount of singing in a village. The name itself actually translates to "sittings" which replaces glamour with utility. Songs, jokes or poems that may interest others may be contributed by anyone and this is done over beer and Snacks at night. Like the other informal social singing that occurs during weddings, festivals or other community celebrations throughout the year.

Inextricably linked to the quality of life, collaborative music playing is as much a culturally defined want for social interaction and catharsis as the desire to provide entertainment.

As a consequence, the Lithuanian musical expression is more viewed as a duty rather than a right. People with folk practices refer to themselves as the custodians of culture entrusted with the duty of transferring, songs, stories and rhythms to the other generations. This sense of custodial duty somehow gives Lithuanian roots music a very ethical tone. They pledge to transmit heritage as a gift and not as a saleable good if cultural experience, constitutive of human identity, is to be carried forward.

Custodial ethics apply to anyone performing music and media and to anyone present in the digital media environment. Many known folk singers acquired repertoire through childhood observation of elder relatives singing the same at family functions or village events. Before they ever stepped foot on the festival stages, they undertook the duties of bringing and passing the tradition via catechist immersion. Subsequently popularizing themselves internationally with Grammy-awarded albums, these stars bear early communal education even when they go mainstream. For those presented with firsthand experience of the two stars in a light stage, their career exemplifies the generosity of cultural heritage linking all Lithuanians as successors to such traditions Lithuanian music is Lithuanian for everybody, regardless of who's it is or how widely recognized.

Lithuanian folk music is an exciting process of welcoming and encompassing the past even as walking into the future. Today modern music concerns brand new discoveries and elaborations, and songs Nguyen deploy traditional ancient tunes which exist in blood spilling. As with most subgenres of role-playing, heritage continues to build on the past and keep works active in creation and presentation rather than placing them in museum form. Lithuanian music unfolds successively with added chronological sequences that enhance the top of another In the historical line.

In essence, it has to do with delineating spheres of relation – between epochs, regions, people and actual or fictitious groups. Folk arts are traditional markers, stating the relation to ancient Baltic culture as modern composition indicates future music.

Passionate words connect internal and external geographies regardless of space divide and temporal differences. Wherever Lithuanians may go outward or inwardwards in space and time, music reminds them of the route back and the web of sound signifiers that demarcate this tiny strip of soil.

Even during oppressions that seemed to endanger the very culture's existence Lithuanian music remained as a vector of identity and unity. Songs went through hidden spaces to preserve ethnicity through darkness to light – a score for the rebirth narrative of a nation. Current freedom has opened the possibilities for free musical worship exponentially creating more opportunities for extended new artistry. Still, contemporary artists do not deny their obligation to take external impressions back to Lithuania and transform the foreign experience through the disparate Lithuanian perspectives that filter outside experiences through a broadly conceived process of creating novel local versions. The nation's song resonates beyond the audio wallpaper singing soul for an international people perpetually returning to the artistic geographic origin.

Wherever resonant, the unquenchable themes indicate/synchronize charts to home. The climbing pitches are the backbone of a living, breathing country that'll hold Lithuanians together, no matter which part of the world they may be in or what era they may be from. Smelling of the ancient wood, early morning birds' singing, rhythms of the rains and traditional prehistoric folk's know-how, this music opens the Lithuanian soul profusely all the time. Had they been transferred orally, from lips to ears by hands instruments and technology these timeless songs would have turned listeners into first-degree unmediated ontological access to culture.

Origins of Sound

The roots of Lithuanian folk music are very much tied to the prehistoric time when the founding inhabitants of the land started to build simple musical instruments and vocal customs. The results of archaeological research show that the early inhabitants of Lithuania depended on nearby resources, such as wood, bone, and stone, to create basic tools. Their essentially uncomplicated design made these tools important to both the cultivation of musical expression and the establishment of cultural identity.

A kanklės, a zither that remains in use today, is one of the most ancient instruments known in Lithuania. It is thought the kanklės started in the Baltic region and have been an important component of Lithuanian folk music for many years. By and large, this tool consists of a wooden resonator topped with elastic strings that produce a pleasant sound when plucked. Along with its entertainments, the kanklės also carried spiritual meaning, contributing often to rituals and ceremonies.

Indeed, another ancient tool is the birbynė, shaped from either wood or bone into a pipe. Derived from the birbynė is a haunting, ethereal music, which was regularly employed in funerals and religious ceremonies. The simple design of the instrument along with the natural components in its assembly highlights the close relation of early Lithuanians to their ecosystem.

Research has unearthed the skudučiai, a form of pan flute, at a range of archaeological sites in Lithuania. Made either from reeds or hollowed wood, skudučiai generates a variety of sounds that enable you to construct elaborate melodies. In situations that often involve groups, the instrument played a key role in creating loyalty and a united cultural identity for the early groups in Lithuania.

Lithuania's regional landscapes of dense forests, extensive plains, and an abundance of rivers and lakes have played a large part in the historical development of folk music. Long ago, melodies usually adopted the continual rhythm of nature, representing everything from the seasonal shifts to the typical rhythm of dawn and dusk. Look at Dainos, or folk songs, which consistently illustrate the brilliance and strength of nature through a combination of themes, including love, work, and environment, in descriptions of the natural world.

Substantial input to Lithuanian folk music has its roots in the ancient rituals and traditions. A lot of these traditions drew their origins from pagan practises and beliefs, which preceded Christianity's arrival in the area. During the Kupolinės festival, those celebrating the summer solstice express traditional music and dance that honor both the sun and how fruitful the land can be.

Representing the finish of winter and the advent of spring, the Užgavėnės festival illustrates a different way in which traditions of ancient times have affected folk music. While here at this festival, participants take part in clothing and ceremonies designed to dismiss the winter spirits and bring in the new season. All through Užgavėnės, the animated and joyful songs convey a happy delight about the arrival of spring.

We can observe the effect of ancient traditions in the practise of sutartinės, a unique kind of polyphonic singing from Lithuania. It is generally the case that women carry out sutartinės, which entail sophisticated harmony alongside elaborate rhythm. In usual circumstances, the main function of the music is to accompany celebrations for weddings, funerals, and agricultural rites. The detailed design of sutartinės illustrates both the deep cultural insight and musical capacity of the performers, alongside the value of shared singing in Lithuanian folk traditions.

In addition to the functions of natural landscapes and historical traditions, the progress of Lithuanian folk music has received substantial direction from the relationships among different ethnic groups and cultures. The Baltic region has a deep cultural exchange history, greatly influenced by its neighbouring countries Poland, Russia, and Germany. The interactions have improved Lithuania's musical heritage while also bringing new musical instruments, melodies, and styles to the folk collection.

Dancing the polka, a cheerful form beginning from Central Europe, Lithuanian communities have taken on and adapted it according to their existing musical traditions. At happy occasions and nuptials, the polka has risen to be a well-liked dance, primarily with musicians embedding their personal interpretations into the sound and beat. The characteristics that make Lithuanian folk music capable and reactive become obvious through cultural exchange, which also supports its ongoing transformation and growth.

Lithuanian folk music has its beginnings in prehistoric times; we should emphasize the evolution of instruments relative to neighbouring environmental traditions. Just a few of the instruments that have helped build the abundant and varied musical legacy of Lithuania are the kanklės, birbynė, and skudučiai. MMusi Lithuanian folk music has flourished and survived due to the relationships among multiple civic and tribal cultures, which have played an important role in its development.

The Medieval Melodies

During the years from 1236 to 1795 that made up part of the Grand Duchy of Lithuania, important cultural and political development took place. Considered at its heights, encompassed a wide area from the Baltic to the Black seas and was a rich mix of distinct cultural characteristics. Many years ago, that event created Lithuania's musical identity through a combination of local traditions with external stimuli. This era saw one of the most impressive changes in the development of courtly music. Judges within the courts of the Grand Dukes viewed musicians, poets, and artists as primary centers of cultural life.

Participants at formal music rituals usually observe proficient musicians skilled in a variety of instruments including the lute, harp, and basic string instruments. Classified by its extensive and polished qualities, the music fit the objectives and activities of the leading elite. The Catholic Church had a major effect on the development of mediaeval Lithuanian music. The cultural scene of Lithuania received a major enhancement after the religious music became important following its Christianization at the close of the 14th century. As educators, churches alongside monasteries played an important part in the demonstration of music. Thanks to their addition of Gregorian chants, hymns, and liturgical music, music diversity in that period experienced an increase. In this time, the interaction observed between religious and secular music gained particular importance. Many melodies drawn from different religions were adopted for secular purposes, and the other way around. Generally, the giesmė was sung during religious ceremonies and at exciting public celebrations. The correspondence between sacred and profane music points out the flexible characteristics of musical traditions that were characteristic of medieval times.

Not just confined to churches and monasteries, the religious musical practises of the mediaeval era took place. It moved through the more extensive cultural environment, where it shaped the development of folk music. Much of religious music has adapted and become part of the folklore of folk songs, illustrating the considerable link between sacred and profane experiences.

An important case of changing is the kolyada, a Christmas tune that combines religious aspects with conventional folk heritage. During the Christmas celebration, kolyada performances unite homes with religious and joyful songs. The kolyada illustrates the method by which religious songs were tailored and combined into routine living, forming a part of the larger folk tradition.

Folk traditions have greatly benefited from the major role that courtly music played. The detailed practices in music and instruments of the court regularly influenced the general public, modifying their local music behaviors. The use of lute and harp in courtly music created an atmosphere that fostered similar instrument creation in the folk traditions of kanklės and smuikas (a fiddle).

Examples of the blend between courtly and folk traditions are the vilkolakio Dainos, or werewolf songs. The wealthy and the middle class both enjoy these songs, which generally feature legendary beings together with supernatural occurrences. The vilkolakio Dainos illustrate the way in which courtly styles and themes were reinvented and included into a larger folk music tradition, resulting in a richly varied musical heritage.

In addition, the mediaeval time frame saw the growth of a unique musical notation for Lithuanians. Found in sacred manuscripts, the neumenai were adapted for the needs of secular music. Due to the notation method, managing and presenting musical data was simple, which backed the widespread sharing of novel melodies and new music styles across the Grand Duchy.

It was imperative to this period that minstrels and musicians travelled. While on their excursions, these entertainers showed off a considerable musical assortment covering themes derived from both holy and mundane subjects. Minstrels served as the chief means by which new musical styles and instruments spread, thus creating a community around music throughout the Grand Duchy.

The composition of ethnicities and languages in the Grand Duchy of Lithuaniastrengthens the visibility of its multicultural nature. This specific sort of cultural variety played an important role in the growth of music in Lithuania. Exchanges with neighbouring populations, the Germans, Russians, and Poles, have added new instruments and musical styles to the music played by Lithuanians.

In this context, the Polish effect was particularly remarkable. The instrumental traditions of Poland, notably the lira (hurdy-gurdy) and the dulcimer, have been taken up and personalized by their Lithuanian followers. The special and successful musical heritage found in Lithuania is the result of cultural fusion.

During that time, the impact of the East was obvious. The Grand Duchy's growth into what is today Ukraine and Belarus introduced Lithuanian musicians to traditions of Eastern Slavic culture. Featuring the balalaika and the gusli has created totally novel textures and sounds for Lithuanian music.

Noting musical practices from Western Europe was just as important in the interactions. The exchanges between the Grand Duchy in trading and diplomacy with Europe caused the transmission of musical distinctives and instruments. As a case in point, the reception of the organ in Lithuanian churches demonstrated the results of Western European musical styles. The cultural exchange exposes the varying and flexible personality of Lithuanian music across the Medieval era.

In the time of the Middle Ages, musical guilds and experienced musicians became visible. The guilds existed as organizations of performers in charge of both managing and promoting musical pursuits. The growth in guilds led to important improvements in musical education combined with the ongoing practice of music.

An important guild was the cechas (guild) of the trumpeters. A skillful musician was every trumpeter who played an important role in both sacred and secular events. Long associated with power and authority, the sound from the trumpet has usually communicated information about notable moments and messages. The trumpeters' guild supported both the better performance of music and the conservation of old melodies and techniques handed down through the ages.

One of the essential musical unions was the lutists' guild. The players of Lutists were capable with the lute, an instrument with stringed features that found favor in court life and among the people. Not just did the lutists' guild work towards musical literacy and promoting knowledge sharing, it also increased the musical heritage of Lithuania.

The activities of skilled musicians in conjunction with the founding of musical guilds gave rise to support for musical notation and theory. For the advantage of coming generations, musicians began the practice of recording their compositions in addition to their techniques. The purpose of these records was to secure Lithuanian music, promising that traditional melodies and styles would carry on for the future.

The mediaeval era formed the basis for what became contemporary Lithuanian folk music. The combination of cultural externalities together with innovations in musical guilds and skilled musicians has produced a unique and varied musical tradition, which has engaged intimately with religious and courtly music. Many Lithuanian folk music melodies and instruments from the mediaeval era are essential to the music of today. The kanklės, rooted in the mediaeval period, is still one of the most important instruments in the music of Lithuanian folk. At festivals and celebrations today, the sutartinės, which is a kind of medieval polyphonic singing, reflect how contemporary society would adapt to traditional medieval melodies. In the medieval period, it's obvious that mixing domestic cultural aspects with foreign influences resulted in a unique Lithuanian musical identity. This sonic identity has developed continuously, revising itself to fit new cultural and historical settings, all the while securing a solid connexion to its mediaeval origins. During the mediaeval period, Lithuania experienced considerable cultural and musical progress. The impact of courtly, religious, and international influences, merged with the rise of professional musicians and musical guilds, is conveniently understandable in the growth of a detailed and unique musical tradition. Researching the origins of present Lithuanian folk music included a range of aspects, including the application of religious melodies in folk songs along with the growth of both musical notation and theory together with religious and secular music. The mediaeval chapter in Lithuanian music is important, showing the energetic and changeable nature of this thriving musical tradition.

The Folk Revival

An important national awakening in the 19th century resulted in important changes to both the cultural and musical situations in Lithuania. On this occasion, referred to regularly as the Lithuanian National Revival, presented a heightened enthusiasm for Lithuanian language, history, and folk traditions. The aim behind the movement was to respect and recover Lithuanian identity while, especially, resisting forces of foreign domination, notably from the Russian Empire.

The Lithuanian National Revival owed its progress to the 1861 serfdom reform, the escalating wave of nationalism in Europe, and the continuing impact of Romanticism. '

Dr. Basanavičius was a physician, historian, and cultural activist wholly dedicated to furthering Lithuanian culture. Primarily, we must credit the founding of the Lithuanian Scientific Society in 1907 to him, because it was devoted to preserving and improving Lithuanian language, history, and ethnography. Basanavicius made it obvious that Lithuanian folk music plays an essential role in expressing national identity in his description of the framework for its exploration and preservation.

Widely recognized in Lithuania's cultural and political environment, Vincas Kudirka was equally a poet, a composer, and a journalist. Among the anthem's forcefully harmonious and patriotic tone, Lithuanians have turned the symbol into a key emblem of their nationalism and a strong call for independence.

There was a new enthusiasm for folklore studies during the Lithuanian National Revival. Since ethnographers and folklorists consider traditional songs, narratives, and customs critically important indicators of identity, they started their work to document and collect them. The article had importance for the conservation of folk music because it offered the promise that classic melodies and lyrics would continue unchanged moving forward.

During the national awakening, the understanding prevailed that Lithuanian language is essential by linking people culturally and representing their identity. Under the rule of Russia, the long-existing Indo European language of Lithuanian was suppressed, meaning Lithuanian use in both education and public life was severely limited. Usually consisting of writings about folklore, traditional Customs, and folk music, these resources shone a light on their role as representations of Lithuanian identity.

The national awakening received essential support from literature. Jonas Mačiulis and Julija Beniuševičiūtė-Žymantienė are among the writers who have produced materials that honour Lithuanian history, culture, and folk traditions. The lives of average Lithuanians were the subject of many short storeys by Žemaitė, which also emphasised the worth of folk traditions and rural lifestyles.

This time marked a remarkably striking relation between language, literature, and folk music. A large number of writers and bards motivated by the melodies and styles of classic music have affected the development of writing styles in their creative outputs. The image illustrates that a large fraction of Maironis's poetry is related to folk music, which salutes the vital role music plays in Lithuanian literature.

The 19th century saw that both political and social movements shaped the trajectory of Lithuanian folk music development. The country's consciousness arose due to a pressing need to honor and strengthen their identity, in which folk music played an important part. The songs and melodies that have lasted are honored as national icons and a battle anthem against foreign oppression.

In this era, the action related to the smuggling of books in Lithuania stands as one of the most important political developments. As a reaction to the Russian block on Lithuanian language publications, a book smuggling network formed, aimed at the secret distribution of Lithuanian books and periodicals.

The movement to smuggle books treated folk music as an important part. A great deal of the contraband literature contained classic songs and melodies, implying their importance as representations of Lithuanian identity. The typical players in communication and resistance, book smugglers, frequently boosted morale with folk songs while addressing encoded messages.

As a result of 19th century social movements, there was an important effect on folk music. As nationalist feelings intensified, there was a fresh interest in classic customs and traditions of life. The traditional performing of folk music at festivals, celebrations, and throughout political movements started to celebrate Lithuanian identity.

The contribution of women to the national awakening was distinctively high. Women took a central position in the censored book movement, knowingly subjecting themselves to danger in order to provide Lithuanian texts to readers. They played an important part in solidifying and aiding folk music at cultural meetings and functions by presenting traditional melodies and rhythms.

Interest in traditional Lithuanian instruments and musical practises has come back during the national awakening. The acknowledgement of traditional instruments as cultural emblems caused artists along with ethnographers to activate the recording and protection of them. According to the thinking, traditional instruments and procedures would not lose their relevance over time, the main goal was to guard Lithuanian folk music. An important element of Lithuanian folk music for hundreds of years, the kanklės is among the most celebrated Lithuanian instruments. Situated in the region, the kanklės is believed to have surfaced and been used in a massive spectrum of musical situations, from religious originations to secular festivities. During the nation's awakening, the kanklės came to represent Lithuanian identity; musicians and composers started to utilise it in their compositions. During this timeframe, we saw the regeneration of the birbynė, a standard reed pipe produced from wood or bone. The birbynė has traditionally issued a haunting sound that is alarmingly phantasmagorical during funerals and religious ceremonies. The framework of the instrument combined with the natural materials used reflects the close relationship that Lithuanians share with their ecosystem. After the national awakening, the skudučiai, a sort of pan flute, was once more brought to life. Either from wood ridges or from natural reeds, skudučiai permits the construction of pitches that can generate detailed melodies. As part of the festival experience, this instrument was frequently encountered and acted to nurture both cultural participation and a lasting history among Lithuanians.

The return of traditional instruments paired with a growing curiosity in traditional musical practises. Over that duration, the sutartinės —

a kind of polyphonic singing unique to Lithuania — became a symbol of national identity. You will usually see women in groups performing sutartinės, which take advantage of elaborate harmonies and rhythmic structures. Several songs perform a ritualistic or ceremonial duty, generally accompanying both weddings and funerals as well as agricultural festivals.

During the time of national awakening, the rateliai saw a further upswell in popularity as a traditional dance form. The rateliai is the energetic dance name that fuses in traditional music. The performance display showcases complex measures and motions that correspond to the skill and talent of the performers. At cultural events, the respected choice offered by the performances of the rateliai revealed how important traditional dance is to the Lithuanian culture.

The response of the Romantic movement, which started in Europe in the late 18th and continued into the early 19th centuries, was considerable on the rise of Lithuanian folk music. Honored for their renewed interest in nature, emotion, and the past, Romanticists were working to recognize and admire their heritage cultural values. The movement related its activities to the principles of the Lithuanian National Revival to bolster and perpetuate Lithuanian language, history, and folklore.

The poet and playwright, Adam Mickiewicz from Lithuania, was an important figure in the Romantic movement in his home country and was part of the once Grand Duchy of Lithuania.

Quite predictably, the Romantic movement also gave a new impulse to the study of folklore. KM; Ethnographers and folklorists starting to write down the folklore songs, legends and traditions as people realised the role of folklore as an area of the national culture. This work was important because it helped chronicle Lithuanian folk music so that most of the melodies and words of songs would not be forgotten over the years. How this Lithuanian composer and musicians in this period were influenced by Romanticism is discussed here. There is folk music in the Lithuanian context, since Mikalojus Konstantinas Čiurlionis used folk songs in his compositions. Being also a painter, Čiurlionis composed orchestral works in which concept of the unity of arts so eloquently expressed by the Romanticism Moving further. In some of his music pieces Čiurlionis used motives of lithuanian folk songs, melodic and rhythmic structures where integrated in works of

Čiurlionis. For example, in 'In the Forest' as symphonic poem he has put into folk motifs and thus the musical painting of the forest is not just copious, but as filled with details of the phenomenon of the forest as one could want. It also signified for a new generation of Lithuanian musicians and composers who decided to focus on Lithuanian folk music. These musicians realized the role of traditional pieces and definite instruments for the nationality and attempted to use them in their music. Schools and other centers of culture was on of the main source for Lithuanian National Revival publishing as well as staging Lithuanian language, history and folklore. Organizing Lithuanian schools was another important occurrence during this period because future generations of lithuania would receive Lithuanian language and culture education.

It comes as no surprise that the Romantic movement has spurred the study of folklore yet again. Ethnographers and folklorists are now recording the melodies, legends, and traditions as people perceive how important folklore is to national culture. This effort was valuable because it helped to record Lithuanian folk music, so that the bulk of the melodies and words of tunes would not go unremembered with time. The influence of Romanticism on this Lithuanian composer and musicians of the period is the subject of this discussion. Folk music exists in Lithuania's context because Mikalojus Konstantinas Čiurlionis interwove folk songs into his compositions. Given his experience in painting, Čiurlionis developed orchestral pieces in which the concept of the integration of the arts, famously heralded by Romanticism, is clearly demonstrated. Čiurlionis' music pieces contain themes from Lithuanian folk songs, as well as the melody and rhythmic patterns found throughout his pieces. As an illustration, in 'In the Forest' he has woven in folk motifs, making the symphonic painting of the forest abundant and detailed in its reflection of the forest as a phenomenon. This also indicated a choice made by a new generation of Lithuanian musicians and composers to concentrate on Lithuanian folk traditions. Realising the part that traditional music and specific instruments play in identity, these musicians adopted them in their compositions. Publishing studios and culture centres as well as Lithuanian language, history and folklore performances are the main sources of the Lithuanian National Revival. In this period, organising Lithuanian schools became an important action as future Lithuanian generations would obtain education regarding Lithuanian language and culture.

Within the national awakening, the founding of music schools and conservatories turned out to be an important development. For the preservation of traditional Lithuanian music and instruments, it was essential that these institutions played a leading part in facilitating a platform for reviewing and validating folk music. In order to take a prominent role in the Lithuanian musical environment, professional musicians accomplished their key training at music schools and conservatories.

The Lithuanian National Revival made an important and enduring contribution to the culture existing today in Lithuania. The burgeoning enthusiasm for Lithuanian language, history, and folk traditions supported a vibrant and varied cultural environment that includes both literature and art, as well as music and more.

Lithuania's current artists, writers, and musicians represent the results of the folk revival in their work. A lot of these creators look to traditional folk themes and motifs for inspiration, and they add them to their work.

The folk revival has an impact on the music of today's Lithuania. A diverse array of current music makers and composers takes inspiration from the folk music melodies and instruments they add to their original work. The combination of established musical styles with fresh music categories has led to a multitude of complex musical subfields.

The renaissance of folk culture had a marked effect on Lithuanian nationality formation. Lithuanians are feeling a strong sense of cultural pride and unity because of a growth in interest surrounding their language, history, and folk traditions. Having this national identity was important during the move for independence, being a force of unity that extended past regional and political differences.

It is clear from the development of Lithuanian cultural institutions and events how the folk revival influenced them. Celebrating folk music and dance of Lithuania, the Song and Dance Festival was first held in 1924 to underline their importance as items of national identity. The festival celebrates the assorted and rich cultural heritage of Lithuania through participation from choirs, dance ensembles, and performers.

In this time period, Lithuanian folk music still benefits from education in terms of nurture and conservation. Preserving the rich cultural heritage of earlier generations for forthcoming generations is essential work led by schools and cultural institutions in the field of traditional music understanding and promotion.

Between the 19th century and now, the Lithuanian National Revival was an important epoch in the history of Lithuanian folk music. A recommitment to the Lithuanian language, history, and folk traditions has created a solid foundation for the progress of an enthusiastic and inventive cultural setting, which includes literature, art, music, as well as a multitude of others. Lithuanian artists, writers, and musicians today articulate the legacy of the folk revival through their on-going efforts to find creativity in traditional folk themes and motifs. Traditional instruments and practises, the Romantic movement, along with the role of education and cultural institutions all combined to protect and elevate Lithuanian folk music, making certain that this important cultural heritage is passed on to generations to come. Folk music's contribution to cultural imagination remains relevant because of the enduring legacy of the folk revival essential to today's Lithuanian culture.

Dainos

Dainos represent the essential basis of Lithuania's cultural legacy. These works reproduce the basic attributes of Lithuanian identity concerning important events in history, cultural ideals, and how the populace lived. Dainos transcend being simply musical pieces; they serve as reservoirs of collective memory, securing accounts, practises, and ideals which have been handed down from earlier times. The important aspect of Dainos is their capability to show the emotional and spiritual features of Lithuanian people. These pieces demonstrate our ability to reach history, clarifying for us the joys, sorrows, and goals of historical individuals. Lithuanian character's tenacity and creativity find evidence in Dainos, which reveal the abundant cultural diversity of the country. One can trace Dainos beginnings to the pre-Christian time, when Lithuania was a faith that worshipped gods. Generally tied to historical ceremonies and rituals, these early chants revealed a deep religious association the public maintained with nature. In the 14th century with Christianity's arrival, several practises rooted in paganism became part of Christian customs, forming a singular mix of longstanding and modern faiths. During the Middle Ages, Dainos advanced, revealing the way the social and political circumstances in Lithuania were adapting. The music regularly illuminates the kinds of hurdles farmers have to navigate, their relentless ambition for goals, and their hopes for lives that are yet to come. These served to be instruments of resistance to foreign domination, mostly in the time of the

Grand Duchy of Lithuania. Due to the 19th-century national awakening, the position of Dainos increased as cultural activists and intellectuals recognised their function as emblems of Lithuanian identity. We made an effort to accumulate, narrate, and conserve these songs, so that they wouldn't disappear from view for future generations. During that epoch, an increased passion for orthodox music developed and it was important for national revival.

Dainos exist in various themes which reflect different parts of Lithuanian culture and life. Among the most usual topics are love, nature, and work.

Love Dainos are probably the commonest and best loved type of Lithuanian folk songs. These audio files share knowledge about the nuances of human relationships, covering everything from the joy experienced in new romance to the sorrow encountered with loss and breakup. For ages, Dainos—expressions of love that are poetic and metaphorical—have taken their inspiration from the natural world in order to express key emotional experiences.

Nature Dainos illuminate the beauty and strength of the natural world, indicating the tight connexion Lithuanians have with their environment. Many of these tunes represent the changes in seasons, the linked cycles associated with life and death, and the amazing beauty of the natural setting. Our associations of awe and respect with nature Dainos serve to confirm the special, sacred features of the natural world.

Work Dainos reveal the patterns and expectations of daily living, underscoring the integral part that labour plays in the society of Lithuania. This style of music tends to honor the contributions of farmers, fishermen, and craftsmen, in hopes of increasing awareness of what they signify and what they add. Engagement in community and cooperation in Lithuania is visible in the Dainos, who perform active and lively rhythms.

The important function of Lithuanian Dainos includes acting as a communication tool, a celebration medium, and a means for remembrance. Performances take place during a large array of occasions, from both weddings and funerals to festivals and religious ceremonies. In the minds of the Dainos, the current world reminds them of bygone times, encouraging a relationship that builds community.

Wedding Dainos are key to the traditions of Lithuanian wedding celebrations. These tunes honour the coming together of two partners, pointing out the critical importance of family, community, and love. You often find in wedding Dainos complicated harmonies and rhythmic styles that illustrate the joy and excitement usually related to this day.

Join our mailing list to transform your entrepreneurial journey from confusion to clarity. Over and over, these performances concentrate on themes related to death, mourning, and the life that occurs after death, supplying peace and harmony. Because of their sluggish and earnest melodies, funeral Dainos symbolize the important nature of the event.

Festival Dainos are joyful and energising, celebrating the happiness and pleasures of coming together in a community. Often performed at seasonal occasions, these songs take place at the summer solstice (Kupolinės) and the harvest festival (Joninės). Festival Dainos express a joyful spirit, as well as a bright and animated sound when it comes to collective celebration.

Musical forms and styles represented by Dainos illustrate the topics they cover. These melodies expose much about the remarkable musical talent and inventiveness of artists from Lithuania, all of which comes wrapped in complex melodies, exact harmonies, and detailed rhythms. Simple, repetitive melody patterns, are the basis for Dainos, and they are later developed and adorned. Dominant repetition develops a trust and a discernible emotion that claims the listener's fidelity to the rhythm. Pentatonic scales give meaning to their melodies, which are frequently characterized by an unusually disturbing tone. The design of Dainos is commonly confusing, illustrating elaborate and skillful polyphtonic sounds. With its unique polyphonic nature, Sutartinės is an important part of numerous Lithuanian Dainos. Yielded from the musical performance in Sutartinės is an elaborate and detailed harmonic texture consisting of several sung melodic lines. audiences have the opportunity to see the polyphonic style, which illustrates the important function of community singing in Lithuanian culture, especially in sessions conducted by groups of women. The energetic and lively rhythmic organisation of Dainos usually shows the joyful nature of festivity and social unity. A compendium of Dainos features rhythmic diversity along with metre changes, making sure it has a stimulating and energetic effect. This style gains from the use of drums and tambourines in respect to rhythmic complexity. The poems along with the expression of Dainos reveal the original creativity and thinking of the Lithuanian population. Characterized by powerful and appealing visuals, these pieces make mentions of the environment and the experiences we deal with each day. In many different situations, the language considered includes metaphors, similes, and a variety of other poetic practices that unify to create an elaborate and attractive narrative for the listener.

The musical styles and forms shown through Dainos highlight the themes they address. The melodies demonstrate quite a bit about the excellent musical talent and inventiveness of Lithuanian artists, all of which is packaged in detailed harmonies, exact rhythms, and complicated melodies.

At the heart of Dainos is an easy, repetitive melody structure, which will eventually develop and become elaborated. Repetition that is pronounced builds a trust alongside a detectable emotion that seeks the listener's allegiance to the rhythm. The melodies of Pentatonic scales hold meaning, often characterised by an unusually striking sense of unease.

The complexity of Dainos design frequently baffles, demonstrating intricate and competent polytphonic sounds. The distinctive polyphonic quality of Sutartinės makes it an integral element of a variety of Lithuanian Dainos. Yielded from the musical performance in Sutartinės is a rich and elaborate harmonic texture comprising a number of sung melodic lines. The opportunity for audiences to view the polyphonic style illustrates the critical role of community singing in Lithuanian culture, particularly during singing sessions performed by groups of women.

The vibrant energy of Dainos reflects the happy and colorful feelings related to occasions of celebration within community exchanges. A compendium of Dainos presents a rich variety of rhythms and shifts in metre, ensuring a stimulating and lively effect. This style profits from the inclusion of drums and tambourines regarding rhythmic complexity.

In addition to the poems, the Dainos articulate the original creative thinking of Lithuania's people. Distinguished by attractive and persuasive visuals, these pieces bring up both the environment and our daily experiences.

Diverse conditions enable the used language to present metaphors and similes, together with further poetic tools, that lead to a compelling and attractive account for those who follow.

The presentation of Dainos includes communal singing as its important element. These songs emphasize the Lithuanian culture's need for collaboration and community through the spotlight of a community ritual. Engaging in harmony greatly amplifies our ability to build a shared sense of community culture and identity. This presentation shows that sutartinės reflect a Lithuanian vocal practice by which several voices work in unison to produce elaborate, detailed harmonies.

Most of the sharing of Dainos takes place orally, as melodies transition from generation to generation by singing. The oral tradition makes certain that the songs remain intact and additional, so they can develop and adjust over time. Oral transmission offers a chance to incorporate new materials and recent developments, making attention to the flexible and dynamic characteristics of Lithuanian folk music a possibility.

If Lithuanian folk music is to stay relevant, we have to conserve and share knowledge about Dainos. Making the distribution and promotion of these songs happen is vitally important and falls to schools, cultural organisations, and community groups that focus on teaching the next generations about their ancestral cultural heritage. The importance of music schools and conservatories, along with folklore societies, has been to back Dainos and to support the investigation and performance of classical music.

Dainos play a pivotal role in the endurance of current Lithuanian culture. These melodies regularly affect community culture, spurring new creativity and talent amongst emerging creators, artists, and writers. For a considerable period, the themes coming from our music, literature, and visual art have showcased the lasting value of these conventional lyrics.

At present, Lithuanian music shows a strong connexion to the traditions of Dainos. A wealth of today's musicians and composers uses the traditional melodies and instruments from folk music in their musical compositions. We have generated a dynamic and rich musical experience through the combination of classic and modern music that covers a host of genres and styles. Motivated by Dainos and folk, community members in Žalvarinis come to understand their similarities by working these elements into their melodies and generating unique and lively music.

The Dainos tradition is influencing the current landscapes of Lithuanian literature and poetry. A variety of writers and poets use themes, imagery, and poetic styles from these traditional songs and put them into their original work. Though he likes traditional anecdotes and stories, Sigitas Geda indicates the ongoing relevance of Dainos in forming the literary route.

In Lithuania, the visual arts also respond to the customs of Dainos. A lot of artists look to the motivating natural imagery and symbolism seen in these songs for their aesthetic, adding them to their artwork that consists of paintings, sculptures, and numerous other creative pursuits. Antanas Žmuidzinavičius, being the artist, usually stresses the classic folk tales and legends, illustrating their continuing importance in visual art.

Looking intently at particular instances of Dainos along with their effects on Lithuanian society helps to show their cultural importance.

"Aš atėjau į šalį" (I Came to the Village):

This love daina is an affecting study of the hunger and craving that follow new love. There's a wonderful matching of the emotional talents of the vocalist with a song that presents imagery of the environment, reflecting a desire for change. The melody of "Aš atėjau į šalį" is haunting and evocative, reflecting the complexity and intensity of the singer's feelings. The persistent favor and importance of the daina is clear through the work of a variety of artists that have performed and recorded it.

"Žalia giria" (Green Forest):

This nature daina reflects the beauty and force of nature and the deep relationship the Lithuanian people have with their ecosystem. Only with strong visuals that bring attention to both the grandeur and the unknown aspects of the forest can the music achieve its highest potential, together with an emphasis on its sacred natural elements. The melody of "Žalia giria" is lively and energetic, reflecting the spirit of celebration and unity that is central to Lithuanian culture. At festivals and celebrations, the daina performance is directed towards the exploration of its contribution to joy and the chains that connect the community.

"Aš dirbu laukuose" (I Work in the Fields):

This project daina captures the tempos and regimens of everyday life, indicating the central importance of labour in Lithuanian society. These continuing songs stress awe for and the respect for effort, centering on similarities and a comradely belonging among performers. The melody of "Aš dirbu laukuose" is lively and energetic, reflecting the spirit of cooperation and perseverance that is central to Lithuanian culture. Found traditionally in the performance at communal gatherings and festivities, this daina signifies its status as a symbol of cooperative achievement and teamwork.

The future for Dainos in Lithuanian culture looks luminous and positive. Through empowering novel talent—musicians and writers—these longstanding old songs keep their relevance and vitality in today's cultural environment. Preserving and referencing Dainos is vital for keeping Lithuanian folk music alive, creating support for the generations to follow in using them.

In the context of Lithuanian culture, Dainos need education and outreach to succeed. Important to young people's understanding of their ancestors' rich cultural heritage are community organizations, cultural institutions, and schools that lead them in the appreciation of these songs. Dainos' success is dependent on the contributions of music schools, conservatories, and folklore groups; they play a key role in assuring their sustainability and ongoing preservation, therefore backing cultural music analysis and performance.

Dainos in Lithuanian culture depend heavily on innovation and adaptation for their future. As society grows and changes, the traditions of folk music need to change too. Brave and gifted musicians and composers who are alive now are discovering imaginative strategies to incorporate the themes, melodies, and language of Dainos into their music, thereby creating an active and pliable musical environment. The fusion of conventional and cultural elements maintains the resilience of the part as well as its importance in today's culture.

A vital part of how Dainos will evolve in Lithuanian culture is the level of community engagement. Maintaining and extending Lithuanian folk music requires improving the performance and dissemination of these songs. In order to revel in festivals, sing together in the community, and honor celebrations, Lithuanians work towards acquiring their own territory, which enhances a feeling of unity and connexion within their own peoples. In the existing cultural situation, the community's participation in and promotion of Daino performances makes them both vital and active.

Instrumentation and Innovation

The music of Lithuania's folk culture provides an extensive variety of traditional instruments, each of which is distinctive for its particular sound, historical tales, and cultural significance.

Kanklės:

The kanklės constitutes one of the best-known and most important instruments found in Lithuanian folk music. Lithuanians have relied on this old zither instrument for hundreds of years, believed to initially have come from the Baltic area. The kanklės is a wooden soundboard stretched over strings that produces, under typical conditions, an elegant and resonant melodic tone when plucked. Traditionally found in both religious and irreligious milieus, this instrument provides music for rituals, unadorned social exchanges, and festivals alike.

Birbynė:

Crafted either from wood or bone, the birbynė is an aural instrument emitting a sad sound reminiscent of nothingness, widely used in solemn observances. The anthropological study supports belief in the ancient ancestry of the birbynė with evidence gained from archaeology showing its use in antiquity. Instrumental simplicity and the natural components of its design reveal the strong relationship Lithuanians have with their ecosystem. People usually link the birbynė to rituals and religious services, whose serious notes promote feelings of respect and seriousness. Even though hundreds of years old, the birbynė remains important to Lithuanian folk music, and modern performers are reflecting its particular sound in their pieces.

Skudučiai:

A skudučiai is a reed or hollowed wood pan flute producing a range of sounds that can assemble elaborate melodies. From early on in Lithuanian history, the skudučiai is understood to have been a tool used, as documented in historical texts. The practitioners of skudučiai during community festivals and coordinated outdoor events foster a feeling of togetherness and a communal cultural story. The many applications of the instrument and its abundant sound quality make it a widespread favourite among both classic and modern artists.

Dūdmaišis:

Lithuania is the only place where you'll find the dūdmaišis, a special bagpipe. This tool includes an animal skin bag filled with air and serves to produce sound through different pipes. People regard the dūdmaišis as having ancient beginnings, mentioning it in archaic historical texts. Though it dates back far, the dūdmaišis remains pivotal to Lithuanian folk music; today's musicians are adding its special sound to their pieces with greater frequency.

Ragai:

Originated from animal horns or metal, the ragai is a horn that creates a loud resonant sound usually involved in ritual and ceremony. Believers say the origins of the ragai can be traced back to times gone by, illustrated in old textual material. In announcing significant activities, ragai is typically used to indicate everything from weddings to funerals to religious traditions. The alluring, stately and serious quality of the instrument is what draws in aficionados of classical and current music.

Smuikas: Only in Lithuania exists the smuikas, a one-of-a-kind fiddle. The belief is that this device comes from the Baltic area and has been crucial to Lithuanian musical culture for hundreds of years. An average smuika comprises a wooden body coated in strings that, when arced, give off a lovely resonant tone. Used both inside and outside religious settings, the instrument figures in rituals, uplifting moments, and average social occasions. The true advantage of the smuika is its flexibility; able to generate a wide variety of sounds and melodies, it can move from easy and soothing audio to exciting and active beats. The Traditional Significance of Musical Instruments. Traditional Lithuanian instruments represent cultural importance that is much greater than just their instrumental functions. These instruments illustrate emblems of national fundamental identity by revealing the history, ideologies, and cultural values of the Lithuanian people. Connected most often to particular rituals, ceremonies, and celebrations, they carry out an important duty in the maintenance and sharing of cultural heritage. Lithuanian instruments—traditionally—find their use in pontifical and ritual contexts, stressing their vital spiritual and cultural roles. The birbynė usually plays at funerals and in ceremonies; its grieving song helps to maintain a serious and respectful atmosphere. The intention of the ragai is to declare important occasions such as weddings and spiritual ceremonies, through its persuasive sound that represents authenticity and power.

At community gatherings and celebrations in Lithuania, you will find traditional instruments playing, which consolidates a collective cultural heritage and community feeling among Lithuanians. At festivals and celebrations, the kudumais is important, generating a unique sound that adds extra dimension to the hearing experience.

In both common life and work, the traditional Lithuanian instruments are emphasized, pointing out their practical and functional importance. Activities that form part of everyday life, such as working in the field or sitting by the fire, frequently accompany the kanklēs. The smuikas supports not just spiritual rituals but also secular gatherings for celebrations and consistent meetings. The application of these implements in routine life and at work stresses their function as emblems of cultural identity and important practicality.

The design and application of classic Lithuanian instruments have adapted, symbolising the evolution of the culture, social settings, and technology in their country. A spectrum of elements has contributed to this growth, in particular the contribution by external cultures, the appearance of new musical styles and techniques, and the embracing of new materials and technologies.

Instrumental evolution in Lithuania has closely involved the impact of foreign cultures. Collaborations among Lithuania's Poles, Russians, and Germans have played a part in many musical styles and instruments found in the country's music collection. Much of the richness in Lithuania's musical environment is thanks to the dulcimer and lira from Poland, which have contributed to the development of new styles and methods. The balalaika and gusli traditions of the Eastern Slavs have greatly enriched the sound and instrument collections of Lithuanian musicians.

New music styles along with techniques are central to the change in traditional Lithuanian instruments. Important elements in building a substantial and varied musical heritage consist of the links between religious and secular music, the effects of Romanticism, and the role of both professional musicians and musical guilds. Traditional instruments required modification and invention because of the demands they had to meet resulting from polyphonic singing styles like sutartinės, to manage the complex harmonies and rhythms of those songs. As a result of new polka and waltz musical trends, Lithuanian musicians have broadened their instrument and sound selection.

The arrival of novel materials and technologies has significantly influenced the growth of traditional Lithuanian instruments. New materials released, for example, synthetics and metals, made it achievable to develop instruments that are both longer-lasting and adaptive. As an example, the utilisation of electronic amplification has permitted typically quiet instruments, like the kanklės and the smuikas, to resonate in larger auditoriums and to engage a more extensive audience. Digital recording technology has supported the conservation and distribution of traditional music, making certain that these important cultural artefacts resist disappearance over time.

The traditional aesthetic of Lithuanian instruments reveals the social practises and cultural beliefs of the people. As part of musical creation, this equipment plays a dual function; it also represents the traditions, history, and lifestyle of the Lithuanian people.

The architecture of many traditional Lithuanian instruments illustrates the strong connexion the Lithuanian people have with their natural surroundings. Employing natural resources alongside wood, bone, and animal skin tells us of the key role nature has in Lithuanian culture. For instance, because of their tight bond with the natural environment, the birbynė comes from either wood or bone. Lithuanian cultural importance in both hunting and animal husbandry is evident in the ragai, which is produced either from animal horns or metal. In traditional musical instrument development, the employment of these organic elements highlights the cultural value of the natural environment and the critical requirement for sustainable lifestyles.

The design of standard Lithuanian instruments represents the vital value of community and cooperation within Lithuanian society. A great many of these instruments are conceived for shared play, which creates an aura of indivisible togetherness and a rich shared cultural heritage for the performers. Both joy and energy fill festivals and gatherings because of the cheerful sounds created by the skudučiai. At festivals and celebrations, the dūmmaisis builds an intricate and detailed musical environment via its specific sound. Instruments used during community and celebratory gatherings demonstrate the critical importance of community and teamwork, along with the important requirement to join forces and share life's both highs and lows.

The cultural value of ritual and spirituality in Lithuania is vibrantly reflected in the designs of traditional Lithuanian instruments. Different instruments take part in ceremonies and rituals, directing attention to their vital cultural and spiritual importance. Within spirit ceremonies and funerals, the birbynė usually brings a quality of sorrow that encourages seriousness and respectfulness. The ragai instrument indicates to the public important moments, especially weddings and important events, through a loud noise that stresses their significance and the role of the speaker. When we find ourselves in moments of spirituality and ritual, these instruments express our cultural value of spirituality and suggest our important responsibility to value the sacred features of our daily lives.

The innovation and adaptation tradition are distinctive features of Lithuanian folk music, and today's musicians use their inventiveness to embed traditional instruments and sounds into their music. A melting pot of historical and modern forms has generated a detailed and vibrant structure of musical diversity throughout assorted genres and methods.

Artists in Lithuania are suitably meshing historical and current music styles, producing an energetic and varied musical environment now. The direct incorporation of folk into their rock music represents an interesting part of their sound; they manipulate conventional instruments such as the kanklės and smuikas into their music. The project Atalyja merges the melodies of conventional Lithuanian folk music alongside electronic and experimental audio, creating a rewarding and special audio experience. A fusion of tradition and inventive music generates a synthesis of functional benefits and energy in Lithuanian folk music, pointing out the lasting significance of classic instruments and what they symbolize.

Lithuanian composers of today are discovering fresh and original means to merge traditional instruments into their musical pieces. One of the regular practices for Giedrius Kuprevičius, the composer, is the addition of classic Lithuanian instruments, such as the kanklės and birbynė, in both his orchestral and chamber works. Rūta Vitkauskaitė has produced a thriving and productive music scene by fusing together Lithuanian folk rituals and modern classical and experimental music. Today in Lithuania, traditional instrument-centered musical styles reinforce their vital and longstanding importance and relate them to the Lithuanian musical context.

Current musicians in Lithuania are exploring pioneering new ways to renovate and change traditional instruments, creating distinctive and fascinating sounds as a result. Embodying musical traditions of Lithuania creatively, the musician Andrius Mamontovas produces rock and experimental music. The experiments in combination with the inventiveness among today's musicians in Lithuania lead to an enduring evolution and adaptability of traditional instruments, which illustrate their fundamental and vital importance in current society.

Lithuanian music is seeing encouraging and radiant prospects for instrumentation and innovation. Right now, creators are merging accepted instruments and sounds in their artworks, which underlines the important impact and current relevance of these instruments. The interweaving of historical musical forms with new ones, the regular use of traditional instruments within emerging music, and the refinement of skills among existing musicians are all elements of the current transformation and growth in traditional instruments.

The future will see that instrumentation and innovative music in Lithuania greatly depend on outreach and education. The responsibility of communicating cultural inheritance to upcoming generations is an important charge for schools, cultural institutions, and community groups, who are looking to set the mood for traditional instruments. The progression and promotion of traditional instruments is dependent upon the fact that music schools, conservatories, and folklore societies have established an environment for research and performance.

Lithuania's instrumentation and innovation will count on the importance of collaboration and exchange with regard to the future. Through the efforts of artists from many nations, Lithuanian musicians create an important area for creative and innovative expression that cultivates original musical techniques and styles. Lithuanian musicians participate in international idea exchange and the promotion of their music while attending festivals, collaborative ventures, and culture activities around the world.

An important key factor in the future of instrumentation and innovation within Lithuanian music is technological innovation. The presentation of novel materials and technologies along with electronic amplification and digital recording creates exciting and unexplored routes for the transformation and evolution of traditional instruments. Utilisation of these technologies assures the ongoing development and flexibility of traditional instruments, highlighting their ongoing relevance and vigour in the current landscape.

The use of instruments and innovation has long been a defining character of Lithuanian folk music; today's musicians are busy finding original and creative ways to blend traditional instruments and sounds with their music. Traditional Lithuanian instruments incorporate cultural values and social practises of the community, stressing the critical role that nature, community, and spirituality play in Lithuanian society. Linked forces, including cultural impacts from around the world, the rise of new music trends and strategies, and the existence of modern materials and advanced technologies, have played a role in the growth of instrument design and application. Design of instruments embodies cultural beliefs and social customs that keep traditional instruments important and dynamic in the world of music today. The combination of older and existing musical genres, adding traditional instruments to current tunes, and the original and inventive practises of today's artists all support the ongoing change and adaptability of traditional instruments. Lithuania is currently at a good point in its instrumentation and innovation space, thanks to the key role of education, collaboration, and technological innovation in preserving and promoting traditional instruments. As critical and lively instruments, they will occupy a position in the cultural musical tradition of Lithuania, stressing its rich heritage of culture and the adaptable and energetic characteristics of its folk music.

Dance and Rhythm

Lithuania's folk music is the central influence on their cultural identity, enriched and advanced by traditional dancing. Merging musical expression with dance forms a vibrant and interesting cultural basis that highlights the historical traditions, views, and practices reflective of Lithuanians. Dances, according to Lithuanian customs, move past simple gestures; they reflect cultural identity and uncover the basic principles and values that characterize the Lithuanian community.

The melodic designs and beat patterns of Lithuanian folk music offer the starting point for standard dances. In a variety of cases occurring at festivals, celebrations, and gatherings, these dances add to a feeling of community and a common cultural heritage. A sophisticated and elaborate cultural experience results from the relationship between music and dance, which illustrates the key function of both artistic forms in preserving and tarting Lithuanian cultural heritage.

Cultural life within Lithuania is highly dependent on dance, acting as a way to express ourselves, find joy, and keep memories alive. There is a vast repertoire of events covering performance of traditional dances in all contexts including weddings, funerals, festivals, and religious celebrations. These dances create an atmosphere of continuity and connexion that ties the present to our history and enhances community and a feeling of belonging.

Traditional ceremonies at Lithuanian weddings involve wedding dances. The stress continues to be on major themes related to love, family, and community through illustrating the growth of the relationship between two people. Almost always, the significant beats in wedding dancing reflect the celebration and joy inherent in the occasion. See the Rateliai, an important wedding dance which reflects the giftedness and agile movements of the performers. Routinely armed with the kanklės and smuikas, Rateliai consistently present traditional music which creates a sophisticated and detailed soundscape.

Those dances performed at funerals are grave and thoughtful; they function to comfort and soothe in times of loss. Ultimately, these dances handle themes involving death along with grief, along with the peace and understanding that follow. Funeral dances comprise serious and sorrowful melodies coinciding with the real, serious nature of the situation. This piece functions to illustrate by presenting a glad view of life and death, expressing peace and hope. Moreover, this dance usually happens to traditional music, which has the birbynė and ragai offering a sober and moving backdrop.

The vigour and dynamism of festival dancing honor the delight and joys that come from connecting with a community. During annual festivals, such as the summer solstice (Kupolinės) and the harvest festival (Joninės), there are typically these dances. Thanks to the lively setting, dances can join the joy of interdependence and holiday fun through their melodic and rhythmic flavors. Due to the song's liveliness and festive lyrics, the Joninės daina (St. John's Day Song) is a widespread selection at the summer solstice festival. CHIRP Podcast often teams up with traditional music, where instruments including the skudučiai and dūdmaišis make a complex and layered musical environment.

A wealth of cultural meaning extends way beyond the movements in traditional Lithuanian dances. As emblems of national personality, these dances mimic the history, religious ideas, and cultural aspirations of the Lithuanian public. In general, they fulfill an important responsibility in keeping and sharing heritage related to key rituals, festive happenings, and ceremonial celebrations.

Lithuanian cultural and religious dances are visible in the context of rituals and ceremonies. The Kupolinės šokis (Summer Solstice Dance) is part of the summer solstice festival, honouring the impressive and beautiful aspects of nature. In regular situations, the movements of the dance comprise traditional music, thus enhancing and altering the acoustic environment with the kanklės and smuikas. These illustrations note that in the ritual and ceremonial context, they heighten awareness of their vital function as cultural identity and spiritual symbols.

At the community assemblies and in the course of celebrations, traditional Lithuanian dances reinforce a spirit of being one and a common cultural heritage throughout Lithuanian groups. Enthusiastically beat out and energetic, Rateliai typically generates an atmosphere filled with joy and happiness during assemblies of cheer. At festivals and celebrations, the Joninės daina helps to build multilayered and unique musical ambiances thanks to its special sound. At community festivals and celebrations, these dances demonstrate their features, revealing them as representations of cultural heritage and a community identity.

In regular activities and careers, traditional Lithuanian dances have relevance that shows their practical and functional value. As a case in point, Aš dirbu laukuose (I Work in the Fields) is usually performed while people are working in the fields, its energised and joyful sound creating feelings of happiness and excitement. The Sutartinės šokis (Polyphonic Dance) serves in religious and secular settings, accompanying practises, festivities, and everyday meetings. These dances are important in ordinary life and at work because they show their status as indicators of cultural identity and as useful tools.

Over the course of changes in cultural, social, and technological spheres in the nation, Lithuanian dance styles and techniques have developed. This change, encouraged by a host of elements, has opened the doors to new cultures, musical styles, and technologies along with new materials.

Development in traditional Lithuanian dances has been much impacted by foreign cultures. The conversation with close Poles, Russians, and Germans generated new dance styles and methods that became part of how Lithuanians dance. Central European polka and waltz inform our understanding of their effects on the Lithuanian dance scene, leading to both new dance styles and techniques. Dances arising from the khorovod (circle dance) and other dance traditions from Eastern Slavic culture have influenced the options available to performers in Lithuania.

Lithuanian traditional dances have changed fundamentally because of the growth of new musical styles and techniques. The synthesis of religious music styles with those secular, bolstered by the results of Romanticism and the advent of expert musicians, has fostered the achievement of dance custom. For the purpose of organizing the complicated harmonies and rhythms found in these compositions, the growth of polyphonic singing traditions, including sutartinės, depended on the transformation and innovation of previous dance traditions. The rolls out of different musical styles including the polka and the waltz has increased the dance options for Lithuanian performers.

Materials and technological advancements have played an important part in developing traditional Lithuanian dance. Within dance costumes, new materials like synthetic fibres and today's footwear enable the emergence of options that are more durable and optimised for versatility. New technologies such as electronic amplification and digital recording have generated more opportunists for Lithuanian dancers. As a clarifying example, electronic amplification has made it feasible for parks, public squares, and cavernous theaters to carry out traditional dances while drawing in more people. By allowing us to document and share traditional dances, time-based digital recording helps to sustain the meaningful qualities of significant cultural artifacts.

The dress and movement of traditional Lithuanian dances illustrate the cultural ethics and social traditions of the population. What's more, these steps depict cultural symbols that reflect the historical, philosophical, and lifestyle characteristics of the Lithuanian people.

Many traditional Lithuanian dances showcase styles and techniques that emphasise the relationship the Lithuanian people have with their environment. Feataturing natural imagery and symbolism, these dances emphasize the important part nature plays in Lithuanian culture. The Kupolinės šokis celebration honors both the spirit and lovely beauty of nature combined with joyful music that conveys a happy spirit and enthusiasm. The Joninės daina concentrates on the sacred meaning of the environment to illustrate both its greatness and the puzzles it poses. Experience indicates that these natural elements have been integral to extended dances that reflect our cultural value of nature and the requirement for compatibility with the environment.

In Lithuanian folk dances, those extra movements illustrate the basic value of community, teamwork, and tradition characteristic of Lithuanian culture. Most of these folk dances are normally choreographed to involve large groups of dancers and that brings unity and togetherness in the dancing group. For example in the Rateliai that is usually danced at weddings or other festive occasions, vigorous fast motions are integrated in dance symbolizing communal festivity joy. The Sutartinės šokis can be performed as an introduction or intermezzo for religious ceremonies, weddings, other festivities and regular everyday village meetings. The cultural values of these communities are illustrated through their dances, which celebrate kinship, oneness, and a lucky frame of mind regarding collaboration among multiple projects.

Besides, the forms and the materialisation of the classical Lithuanian dances portray the sacredness of Lithuanians' religious sphere and the roots of their bond with spirituality. References A place in sacred rituals and ceremonies has been claimed by lively dances as a way to show the cultural value placed on the spiritual factor of life and the effect of nature on daily life.

In addition, Lithuanian Folk Dance introduces the practice of continuity and ingenuity with the present dancers enhancing the original ideas of ethnic dance styles and movement patterns to enrich different new, energetic representations of arts. Such a combination of traditional and postmodern trends has resulted in the formation of the great and various context of Lithuanian dance space, which encompasses a vast spectrum of dance genres. Lithuanian folk dance continues therefore to be an active, progressive aspect of cultural activity.

Right now, it looks like Lithuanian dancers are exploring original and inventive ways to bring together old dance styles with new ones, consequently activating a vibrant and diverse dance community. Serving as a model, the Aura troupe mixes classic Lithuanian folklore presentations with today's artistic and dramatic influences to form a new and convincing performance. Those involved in the events perform folk dances, such as Rateliai and professional Sutartinės šokis, all while acknowledging folk elements along with current trends and unveiling ornate theatrical movements. The combination of old and new guarantees the continuous organic and dynamic character of Lithuanian folk dance into the contemporary world, emphasizing the continued importance of traditional centuries of traditions and traditions. Lithuanian Choreographers are also now looking for new, inventive ways of integrating traditional dances into their programs. In many of her modern works, Gintarė Ščogolevaitė incorporates the Kupolinės šokis and Joninės daina into a thickly layered performance. When using age-old dances and employing contemporary methods and theatrical elements alongside them, she emphasizes their relevance and vigour to be guaranteed their presence on the Lithuanian dance stage. Contemporary Lithuanians Dancers are also attempting some traditional as well as experimental methods of evolving and changing traditional dance forms for creating new and innovative performances. Their interpretations of aerial dance and movement with lifts develops from such folk dances as the Rateliai and Sutartinės šokis. Functional wholistically complex systems that purposefully affect traditional dances communicate their fundamental significance and steadfast evolution in the present world.

The dynamic of the role of dance and rhythm in the modern Lithuanian culture might be identified through modern interpretations of various dance forms by modern Lithuanian companies and choreographers.

The professional Lithuanian dance company Aura is known for its interpretation of the Lithuanian folk dances, Rateliai and the Sutartinės šokis in modern and theatrical manners. Their special performances have received devotees proving the present day requirement of conventional dances.

In the same way, Gintarė Ščogolevaitė performs Kupolinės šokis and Joninės daina as elements of modern dances along with other modern oriented choreographies. Her shows are compelling and have won her praise from critics observing that tradition plays a crucial role in today's art.

The Low Air Dance Company also performs aerial dancing in combination with the lithuanian folk dances like Rateliai, Sutartinės šokis. Their ability to combine the traditional and modern, has made them popular, as it proves that even in today's society people love traditional dancing.

This is the future of the dance and rhythm in Lithuanian culture hope and opportunities it has began to glow. Choreographers and dancers today remain unfazed in looking for new ways of incorporating traceable dance forms and movements into their dance, to make them relevant in the present day society. A mixing of contemporary and traditional dance styles, combined with the inclusion of folk dances in modern forms, are some of the explanations for why cultural dance practices are never quiescent. Lithuania's dance and rhythm continuity is largely thanks to educational and promotional efforts. In order to tie the current generation to bygone days, educators and civil society organizations are important for maintaining the traditional dance for new generations. The continued con¬servation and presentation of these dance forms would not happen without the learning and performance opportunities available from dance schools, conservatoires, and folklore organizations for students. Friendship and evolution connected to the cultural cross are also important to develop the dance and rhythm part in Lithuanian culture. Exchange between Lithuanian and the rest of the dancers provides rich and valuable source of inspiration and service in bringing new dances into the society. Lithuanian dancers are responding to invitation to international festivals, conferences and cultural manifestations – it is a way of sharing experience, presenting Lithuanian dance performances to the world.

Part of Lithuanian cultural identity is formed by folk music as well as traditions in dancing. These dances are not mere somatic activities - they are the spirit and values of the nation as these dances rekindle the cultural identity through erected representations that invoke importance of the nature, communal and spirituality. As it has been mentioned before, the styles and techniques of the traditional dances appeared and developed in different historical period, which influenced them with the other cultures, or the new kind of tunes, or the new technologies and materials.

In future developments of Lithuanian culture dance and rhythm is going to be and important factor. Culturally acceptable knowledge surrounding the dances underscores their continuity from generation to another. It offers a constant evolution or even concerning traditional and contemporary dancers, possible that enable to draw together and experiment. Even so, today's facilities including electronic aural enhancement and digital recording present huge opportunities for changing and modifying the dances. The syncretism of old and new means that film and dance specifically will emphasize the timeless value of both art forms to the contemporary world. Technology will bring change into the development of the traditional Lithuanian dance while preserving the essence of the dance.

Thus though performed today, Lithuanian dances are not a static recording of historical past. The traditions negation to change and this means that the continuing change will reflect the ongoing nature of the particular culture in question. Music and dance continue equally for today and for tomorrow since the passion to create something and foster the spirit of unity remains eternal in Lithuanian landscapes.

Celebrations

Celebrations and festivals in Lithuania rely heavily on music all year long, enriching ceremonial, ritual, and community gathering occasions that honor the changing of the seasons. In addition to functioning as social gatherings, these festivals reflect Lithuanian cultural identity and stress Lithuanian history, views, and beliefs.

Spring festivals in Lithuania celebrate the feeling of hope and new life, fully aware of the warmth and brilliance that arise after a long winter of calm. At these festivities, classic music mixed with classic dancing occupy a prime position and produce an enthusiastic and energetic musical spirit. Užgavėnės, or Shrovetide, is a festival that celebrates the finish of winter and the start of spring leading into Lent. Thanks in part to traditional kanklės and smuikas, this festival celebrates its vibrant and energetic musical style, which is richly textured. Since tradition, the tunes and dances of Užgavėnės concentrate on ideas pertaining to renewal, fertility, and the fun of successfully finishing tasks.

The festivals of summer in Lithuania reveal the highest point of agricultural work, accompanied by the joy felt in the warmth. At these happenings, the vibrant soundscape and abundant music are a result of the historic melodies and dances present. The midsummer festival of Joninės (St. John's Day) is a celebration that recognises the summer solstice. As would be expected from its playful and energetic vibe, the festival is highlighted by traditional instruments, the skudučiai and dūmmaisis, which create a deep and attractive musical quilt. Both the spirited celebrations and community feeling, as well as the joy of outdoor activities, frequently appear in the music and dance of Joninės.

Lithuanian autumn festivals reflect a feeling of progress and awareness whilst honoring the transition between seasons and preparing for the toughness of winter. Celebrations at these festivals use traditional music and dances as their quiet and inward-looking soundtrack. As a celebration of Vėlinės (All Souls' Day) in the autumn, Lithuanians honour the memory of the deceased. Distinguished by its thoughtful and reflective music, the festival beautifies the night with the birbynė and ragai to develop a supportive and meaningful setting. Usually, the music and the dance of Vėlinės reflect talks about remembrance, loss, and the repetitive character of existence and death.

Festivals that happen in winter celebrate a tone of quietude and reflection, commemorating the tranquil beauty of winter and the cheer of family and home. The festival makes use of its special musical qualities, slower and conducive to thoughtfulness, to honour classic instruments like the kanklės and smuikas in order to build a detailed and lush aural experience. The sounds and movements of Kūčios typically reflect clearly the ideas of family, home, and the joy of winter.

The festivals and observances during each season have importance that goes beyond entertainment and assembly social events. Festivals reflect cultural identity by concentrating on the historical, spiritual, and moral characteristics of Lithuanian people.

In Lithuania, the signifcant spiritual and cultural function through ritual and ceremony is reflected by a diversity of celebrations and seasonal festivals. The festival Užgavėnės marks its occasion through a variety of rituals and events that symbolise the winter being over and the initiation of spring. Usually, in application, these traditions typically consist of lighting effigies, tasting standard meal, and executing classic dances and musical numbers.

Lithuanian seasonal festivals and celebrations help create a sense of community and shared cultural heritage because they are used at gatherings and celebrations for the Lithuanian community. The festival of Joninės marks a series of collective assemblies and celebrations which celebrate the top of the summer season. Sharing traditional performances, nourishing traditional meals, and trading stories and memories is usually a feature of these assemblies. These festivals applied to gatherings for the community and celebrations reveal their representation of cultural identity along with a community spirit.

Celebrations and festivals that occur with seasons reflect their practical and functional importance within both work and daily life. The festival of Vėlinės celebrates with a variety of rituals and ceremonies that venerate those who have passed away. Rituals almost always comprise operations involving cleaning and beautifying tombstones, shining light on candles, and executing traditional songs and dances. Their role as part of everyday ritual and work reveals their function as indicators of cultural identity and as meaningful symbols.

Lithuania's festivals and parties have shifted in recent times in reaction to the changing social, cultural, and technological scenes of the region.

The contributions from different countries have favourably contributed to the growth of seasonal festivals and celebrations in Lithuania. Communication with neighboring cultures led by the Poles, Russians, and Germans has resulted in the adding of additional rituals, ceremonies, and musical styles to the Lithuanian musical collection. Lithuania's holiday culture has expanded with the arrival of Christmas celebrations from Western Europe, which have added fresh rituals and ceremonies to its celebrations. As a result of the traditions of Eastern Slavs, including celebrating Maslenitsa before Lent, Lithuanian communities have a broader range of festival possibilities.

A study of particular festivals and their cultural significance provides insight into the contribution of seasonal festivals and celebrations to contemporary Lithuanian culture.

Joninės (St. John's Day):

Celebrated at midsummer, the festival of Joninės acknowledges the summer solstice. Festschrift characterises its animated and energising music, thanks to traditional instruments such as the skudučiai and the dūdmaišis contributing a full and textured musical experience. According to tradition, the songs and dances during Joninės illuminate important subjects of commemoration, interconnection, and the wonderful joy of enjoying outdoor leisure time. At the festival, it's common for people to listen to both traditional and contemporary music; electronic beats and synthesisers augment the melodies and instruments of the traditional variety. The festival called Joninės has a major effect on cultural life by building stronger ties of harmony and shared cultural heritage in Lithuanian communities.

Užgavėnės (Shrovetide):

Užgavėnės is a festive event before Lent that symbolises winter's conclusion and the coming of spring. The event offers spirited and engaging music, augmented by the kanklės and smuikas, which help sculpt a comprehensive and vibrant audio ecosystem. The songs and dances typical of Užgavėnės usually include a common theme of emotional renewal and fertility. At the festival, the way things are organised typically features a blend of traditional and contemporary dance styles, in which contemporary dance methods and theatrical elements back the traditional melodies and dances.

Vėlinės (All Souls' Day):

The festival Vėlinės is an occasion in autumn dedicated to the remembrance of those who have passed away. The emphasis of the festival is on unhurried music full of considered thinking, created by the birbynė and ragai in a keen and urgent manner. Regularly in Vėlinės performances, songs and dances call to mind remembrance, loss, and the cycle associated with life and death.

During the festival, people typically celebrate by blending classic and novel art, where current sculptures and installations support the traditional practises and ceremonies.

Kūčios (Christmas Eve):

Kūčios is a winter festival that closes the Advent season and starts the Christmas one. Because of its soothing and deliberate energy and musical offerings, the festival champions traditional instruments such as the kanklės and smuikas that combine flawlessly to produce a detailed and lush musical setting. Kūčios' performances usually feature ideas revolving around family, residence, and the benefits of winter. The festival regularly celebrates a variety of cuisine, including traditional and contemporary elements, where modern cooking approaches and ingredients blend nicely with the classic recipes.

The celebrations and festivals that are bright and animated in Lithuania each year celebrate its cultural identity while drawing attention to history, religious outlooks, and ethics. As well as being social occasions, these festivals represent cultural identity and reflect off life. The design and techniques of seasonal festivals and celebrations mirror the cultural values and social practises of the community, spotlighting the importance contained in Lithuanian society for nature, community, and spirituality. A multitude of elements have resulted in the change of seasonal festivals and celebrations, such as adoption from foreign cultures, the appearance of latest musical styles and techniques, and ongoing availability of new technology and materials. Seasonal festivals reflect cultural values and social practises, guaranteeing their ongoing relevance and vitality in today's cultural environment. Integrating traditional assets with new elements, reintegrating standard festivals into updated contexts, and adopting innovative ideas and experiments from existing communities strengthens the flexibility and development of timeless festivals and celebrations. The future of Lithuanian traditions and celebrations looks bright, due in part to both educational efforts and teamwork with technological development, which are necessary for their preservation and the growth of these celebrations. Their historical importance and sustained role give evidence to their continuing relevance in the cultural ethos of Lithuania, illustrating the riches of their cultural heritage along with the adaptability and flexibility of Lithuanian ceremonies and seasons.

Religion and Mythology

Lithuania's folk music strongly associates with its rich array of religious and mythological customs. Preoccupied by routine components, the rich and rhythmic nature, strategies, and topic areas of folk music set up a lively and exciting cultural framework. Throughout Lithuanian spiritual and cultural identity, one can see the connection between religion, mythology, and folk music build a perennial connection to history.

Folk music has experienced a substantial impact from Lithuania's beliefs and practises prevalent before Christianity. The music and dances in ancient pagan rites reflected the powerful spiritual association the community maintained with nature. Initiated to praise the attractiveness and powerful character of nature, the Kupolinės celebration looks to ancient pagan customs. At the festival, the stimulating presentation of old instruments—kanklės and smuikas—provides a deep and rich musical experience. The Kupolinės dances and music serve to illustrate joyful and fulfilling community aspects, including the fun of enjoying time together outside, along with the collective strength we find.

Folk music in Lithuania received new themes and styles when Christianity became established in the 14th century. The appearance of sacred and secular sounds resulted from hymns, chants, and religious services that all included parts of traditional folk music. The highlight of the Christian holiday season, the Kūčios festival, is marked by relaxed and mindful musical tones on the occasion of closing Advent and launching Christmas. The music and dance of Kūčios regularly bring forth themes important to family, home, and the enjoyable elements of winter. The festival usually celebrates food by fusing old and new, where today's culinary techniques and ingredients emphasize traditional dishes and recipes.

Lithuania's rich folklore music is the place to find the country's ancient tales and legends. Traditionally, subjects such as these research the supernatural, the divine, also the heroic, to provide a reverential and marvelous experience. We find that the sutartinės, the special form of polyphonic singing characteristic of Lithuania, often integrate themes and imagery from mythology. In the discipline of sutartinės, the sophisticated musical harmonies and rhythms mean reflections about the divine as well as the supernatural.

The part that religion and mythology play in establishing Lithuanian cultural identity has been serious and lasting. Based on these traditions, there exists a framework for grasping the world that furnishes meaning and purpose that improves the quality of life for Lithuanian citizens. The narrative regarding Lithuanian history and culture develops to the point of further enriching a historical connection to place by using talks focused on religion, mythology, and folk music.

The Lithuanian population has greatly depended upon both religion and mythology for their spiritual and cultural values. These traditions have marked out a way to make sense of the natural environment, the holy, and what it signifies to be human. The religious beliefs of ancient pagans in the holiness of nature have played a part in shaping contemporary environmental ethics as well as our need to live in sync with the natural environment. Lithuanian society has seen moral and ethical evolution with the introduction of Christianity, which has supplied both importance and a life direction.

The traditions and ceremonies of the Lithuanian people owe a substantial debt to religion and mythology. The rituals and ceremonies created by Lithuanians contribute a perception of organization and form to their lives, while celebrating vital life changes and events. The festival known as Vėlinės (All Souls' Day) honours those who have died by being marked by slower, more reflective music. The musical and dance elements of Vėlinės usually tell stories related to remembrance, loss, and the way life and death function. Serious festivals are frequently celebrated with a mix of historical and modern art; modern sculptures and installations fit seamlessly alongside the historical rituals and traditions. There is a considerable obligation owed by Lithuanian society's traditions of storytelling and cultural heritage to the impact of religion and mythology. This tradition has acted as a rich inspiration for both folk music and literature as well as art. Generally speaking, the dainos (folk songs) bring forward mythological themes alongside artwork that bears a resemblance to the old histories and legends of the Lithuanian people.

Lithuania's cultural heritage comprises how religion, mythology, and folk music interact with one another. The bright and full-colour customs of Lithuanian traditional music illustrate the spirit and cultural identity of Lithuanian folk, keeping a link of coherence and historical relevance in place. Cultural identity effectively and continuously progresses because of religion and mythology, changing spiritual and cultural values, rituals and observances, all the while influencing storytelling traditions. As international awareness of Lithuanian folk music increases, dependence on education, partnership, and technological innovation in order to support and advance this unique musical style will become crucial. The ongoing pertinence and financial aid for Lithuanian folk music point to a visible future role on the international music scene, reflecting both the richness of Lithuanian cultural assets and the adjustable and flexible attributes of Lithuanian folk music.

Preservation

Origins of Lithuanian folk music is vital for keeping the relationship with cultural heritage and establishing the identity of its people. As an archive, folk music represents the history, ethos, and traditions of the nation, and echoes the feelings and experiences of ancient communities. The transition and improvement of societies comes with an increased danger of losing or reducing traditional musical practises. Consequently, coordinated action is important to make sure that Lithuanian folk music remains healthy and continues passing on to the next generations.

The identity of Lithuania strongly relies on its folk music. It reflects the special character, history, and beliefs of the Lithuanian people. Upkeeping this music helps to continualize connexions to our past, fostering a powerful cultural identity in today and tomorrow.

In addition, folk music has considerable educational value. The resource gives an understanding of the historical background, beliefs, and daily life of the Lithuanian people. Understanding and learning from folk music helps many to appreciate their cultural heritage better as well as the more comprehensive context of Lithuanian society.

Maintaing folk music greatly contributes to community formation. The appeal of already known melodies and choreography brings in the audience, helping extend a strong community sentiment and a plain cultural identity. Celebrations and performances conducted together create stronger ties in Lithuanian communities and increase a feeling of belonging.

Strategies for the effort to facilitate Lithuanian folk music cover documentation, studies, and community involvement. A wide range of entities, organizations, and individuals is engaged in these projects to keep Lithuania's vibrant musical heritage intact for coming years.

Documentation plays a basic role in preservation. This comprises the approach of recording, transcribing, and storing the heritage characteristics of traditional music, dances, and musical heritage. In this endeavour, ethnomusicologists, folklorists, and cultural institutions are critically important.

Preserving Lithuanian folk music becomes rather hard without education. At schools, universities, and cultural institutes, courses and programmes center around the teaching of traditional musical techniques. Programs of education promise that the next generations comprehend and can gracefully practice folk music. As an authority in offering unique instruction in traditional music, dance, and instrumentation, the Lithuanian Academy of Music and Theatre targets these fields.

Community participation is one more vital ingredient in the success of preservation. Organising events that facilitate coming together to celebrate traditional music as part of festivals, workshops, and cultural performances is a part of this. Projects that value community help make folk music relevant and important by nurturing a sense of ownership and pride in the participants. Every year, the festival Skamba Skamba Kankliai brings together folk musicians, scholars, and enthusiasts who love their craft from both Lithuania and around the world, to celebrate the richness and vibrancy of the nation's music history.

Lithuanian folk music preservation greatly depends on education. Having traditional music woven into educational and cultural institution materials helps to assure that young individuals appreciate and know their cultural background.

Effective education depends on the necessity of producing detailed curricula that contain traditional music. This material aim is to provide students with a totally enlightening view of Lithuanian folk music, including its history, theory, and practice. As an illustration, the Lithuanian Ministry of Education has added traditional music to the national curriculum to help acquaint all students with their cultural heritage.

Effectively teaching traditional music is critically dependent on the training given to teachers. In order to thrive, teachers need to understand the material and be able to support multiple musical practices. The reason teachers remain up to date with their research and teaching approaches is the existence of resources such as professional development support, workshops, and seminars.

For educational efforts to succeed, it is important to engage students in how they learn. As a result of activities that improve engagement and need physical involvement, learning can turn out to be rewarding and entertaining, such as through singing, dancing, and enacting traditional music.

Despite significant growth in both the defense and knowledge of Lithuanian folk music, a range of challenges remains. Looking into these challenges and making use of the current opportunities can support the sustained dynamism of cultural musical practises.

Challenges:

Funding and Resources: It can be hard to obtain adequate resources and financing for preservation and educational programmes. Lack of sufficient financial resources can impair the success of these programmes and narrow their coverage.

Technological Changes: The quickening rate of technological evolution may face difficulties in preserving traditional music. Out of necessity for their sustained relevance, they need to modify and include traditional techniques in modern frameworks.

Generational Shifts: Persuading young people to engage with the conservation and enjoyment of traditional music is fairly complicated. In today's society, it's becoming more difficult to persuade folk music to seem pertinent as cultural ideals and interests change.

Opportunities:

Digital Technologies: Utilizing digital technologies well can both strengthen the conservation of traditional music ideas and enhance their reach. Online spaces along with multimedia resources and digital archives facilitate access to and connection with folk music for a larger community.

International Collaboration: Cooperation with foreign institutions and agencies provides additional understanding and resources for both the promotion and conservation of Lithuanian folk music. Cooperations around the globe can raise Lithuanian cultural heritage on a global scale.

Community Involvement: Mining local communities for input in conservation and educational programs may create a bond that is personal and has cultural pride.

Community-driven programmes and projects might support the maintenance of traditional music and its primary function in our contemporary community.

The cultural heritage and identity of Lithuanians demand the circulation and communication of the fundamental aspects of folk music. The important task of documenting, educating, and engaging the community allows us to guarantee that traditional musical practises will continue Into the future. The Lithuanian Folk Culture Centre, along with the Lithuanian Academy of Music and Theatre and the Skamba Skamba Kankliai festival, show the impact and the critical relevance of these projects. Meeting these challenges requires taking advantage of current opportunities, largely by fostering partnerships at the community level and through digital technologies and international partnerships, which will strengthen the strength of Lithuanian folk music. Lithuania's ability to sustain a unique cultural identity and encourage a closer attachment to a rich heritage in the years ahead will depend on the sustainable protection and advancement of its traditional musical traditions.

Disclaimer

Everything shared in this book should be considered as educational and informative in nature. The author and publisher shall not be responsible for any loss or damage suffered by any reader directly or indirectly through reading of, reliance on, and use of information that only the author and the publisher know at the time of writing this book.

Some of the suggestions given and the approaches recommended in the book may not be applicable to certain circumstances. The author and the publisher shall not be held responsible for any damages caused as a direct result of the use or non-use of the information presented in this book.

It is understood that readers should not rely on it for professional solicitations such as medical, legal, financial, and other related opinions. If any professional help is needed, then advice of a competent professional person should be taken.

The author and the publisher will not be held responsible for direct, indirect, special, or consequential damages or any other costs whatsoever arising from the use of the information present herein in this book.

About the Author

Maher Asaad Baker (In Arabic: ماهر أسعد بكر), is a Syrian musician, author, journalist, VFX & graphic artist, and director. He was born in Damascus in 1977. He grew up with a dream of being one of the most well-known artists in the world, and he has been working hard to achieve it ever since.

He started his career in 1997 when he was only 20 years old. He had a passion for technology and media, and he taught himself how to develop applications and websites. He also explored various types of media-creating paths, such as music production, graphic design, video editing, animation, and filmmaking. He was not satisfied with just being a consumer of media; he wanted to be a creator of media.

Reading was another source of inspiration for him. He was always surrounded by books as a child, thanks to his father's extensive library. He read books from different genres, topics, and perspectives. He read books for knowledge, for wisdom, for entertainment, for enlightenment. Reading stimulated his imagination and curiosity. Reading also developed his writing skills.

He did not start writing professionally until later in his life, as he was busy with other projects and pursuits. But when he did start writing, he proved himself to be a talented and prolific writer. He wrote articles for various newspapers and magazines on topics such as politics, culture, society, art, technology, and more. He wrote books that were informative and insightful. He wrote books that were creative and captivating. He wrote books that were best-selling and award-winning.

He is most known for his book "How I wrote a million Wikipedia articles", where he shares his experience of being one of the most prolific contributors to the online encyclopedia. He reveals his methods, techniques, strategies, and secrets of writing high-quality articles on any subject in record time. He also discusses the benefits and challenges of being a Wikipedia editor in the age of information overload.

He is also known for his novel "Becoming the man", where he tells the story of a young man who goes through a series of transformations in his life. The novel explores themes such as identity, masculinity, self-discovery, love, loss, and redemption. The novel is based on his journey to becoming who he is today.

Copyright © 2024 Maher Asaad Baker